INTO THE RIVER

HOW BIG DATA, THE LONG TAIL, AND SITUATED COGNITION ARE CHANGING THE WORLD OF MARKET INSIGHTS FOREVER

T0020887

INTO THE RIVER

HOW BIG DATA, THE LONG TAIL, AND SITUATED COGNITION ARE CHANGING THE WORLD OF MARKET INSIGHTS FOREVER

TONY COSENTINO

Table of Contents

This book is dedicated to

Alexander Lin Cosentino

Who was born on June 7, 2011.

Preface

I wrote this book because I believe that the successful organization of the future will be driven by a strong Market Insights culture. This belief is grounded in the idea that the consumer voice will become more powerful over time as markets become more crowded with suppliers; and Market Insights, in turn, will be the deciding competitive advantage. This idea has motivated me to spend much of my career in the Market Insights industry and has engaged me in a culture of learning which I enjoy tremendously. At the same time, the insights industry is changing as the broader world of commerce is changing, and where the change used to be incremental and episodic, it is now constant. The philosopher Heraclitus' refrain that *nothing changes but change itself,* is as true in the modern world as it was in ancient times. And certainly change itself is healthy, but only when we take a step back to examine it does change present us with a unique form which we can embrace. It's this form that inspired me to contribute to the discussions already taking place across the industry.

In the foundational research that went into writing this book, I reviewed much current business literature and, in particular, the literature of the insights industry. Many of these books struck me as academic textbooks and "how to" books for designing questionnaires, measuring a brand, or doing market segmentation. On the traditional consulting side, most of the work seemed to be about knowledge management and information-based organizational change. One thing that was frustrating was that many of these books took three to four hundred pages to tell the same story over and over again through not-so-exciting anecdotes or by just repeating the same information but in slightly different ways. What seemed to be missing was a simple book addressing the disruptive changes occurring in the Market Insights world and what professionals in the field might need to know to deal with these changes. With Occam's Razor[1] as a guide, I vowed to keep the book focused, not to repeat myself (too many times), and not to use lengthy anecdotes or case studies. In sum, my aspiration for the book is to give the reader a straight-forward perspective into an important and changing industry and put forth ideas on how to deal with these changes.

As I went through iterations with my editors, the challenge of defining terms kept presenting itself. I attribute this challenge to the nature of change itself and to the disruption occurring in the insights industry. The industry is being broadly impacted as the lines blur between software and research, marketer and researcher, consumer and innovator. Since this did not provide a good enough excuse to my editors, a discussion of a few terms is necessary here. The terms *Market Research* and *Market Insight* are used somewhat interchangeably throughout the industry and throughout this book. (In the industry, the term Market Intelligence is often

---

[1] The idea of Occam's Razor suggests that one should provide the simplest possible solution without being simplistic. (Bertrand Russell similarly suggested that every complex problem has a simple answer, and that such an answer is usually wrong.)

used interchangeably with Market Insights. The terms Shopper Insights and Consumer Insights are often used in Consumer Packaged Goods and Retail.) Where the connotation is more aligned with the definition presented here (i.e. *Market Research is any organized effort to gather information about markets or customers*), I have tried to use the term Market Research. Where the connotation is more aligned with the Market Insights definition here (i.e. *market insight is the understanding of a specific cause and effect in a specific market context),* I have tried to use Market Insights. There may also be some confusion over the terms *insights industry* and *insights function.* When I use the term insights *industry*, I am generally speaking of the entire eco-system of industry suppliers, and in some cases, the definition extends to corporation's internal Market Research function. Furthermore, as the disruptive model takes hold, this eco-system expands to include management consulting and some technology firms. The word *function* is meant as a descriptor of internal corporate insights departments, but the lines are also being redrawn here as marketing and information technology becomes much more integrated with the insights function.

* * * * *

Most importantly, I'd like to thank the people that helped me with this book. Jodi, I don't know that this book would have made it without you. Eric, our discussions and work through the years have provided much of the insight in this book. Mike, you listened and then gave me sound consult. Jim, and Craig, you helped me to understand some of the most complex ideas and forces driving the industry. Sanjit, your early review was quite valuable; you are such an inspiring teacher. Serenella, you are the *uberanalyst* I speak of in these pages. Carlos, you provided the intellectual catalyst to write this book; our worlds are most certainly coming together. To all of my other mentors, and colleagues, you make this industry exciting and fun. To my wife, my parents, and my new-born son, you provide my inspiration and it's your unwavering support and confidence that has allowed me to take on this effort.

Tony Cosentino

October, 2011

Introduction- The Empty Chair at the Table

> You could not step twice into the same river; for other waters are ever flowing on to you.
>
> - Heraclitus

Joe, the COO, and soon to be CEO of the telecommunications provider, US Telco[2], sits at his desk and considers what to do about the bleeding. Churn rates have increased dramatically over the past six months as more and more customers drop off the network. What's worse is that he cannot pinpoint exactly why this is happening. Mike, his right hand in the organization, tells him it's because of network coverage and that the cell towers need to be closer together. He points to a significant correlation between dropped calls and customer churn.

Joe thinks to himself...*That's a huge infrastructure investment not certain to solve our problem.*

Lucas, the head of marketing, shows Joe a model that predicts share stabilization if they roll out fresh service plan structures and new pricing. Of course, this would need to be followed up with an aggressive media campaign. While Joe believes the projections, he remains unconvinced.

---

[2] This story is fictional.

1

Joe noodles the idea...*While new pricing may stabilize share, how is this going to change our longer term prospects? Specifically, how will it impact the profile of our customer base and impact our brand? The street certainly won't like it; lower margins and a brand promise of being cheap. It's like putting a Band-Aid on this wide open wound. It's not good enough.*

Joe considers how the decisions were made in the past. Usually a prioritized list based on the leading impacts to their customer loyalty index (CLI) helped to sort through different scenarios. The company looked at big competitive tracking studies, listened to what people said they were going to do, and took the guidance seriously.

Joe considers these studies...*It seems to me that people don't always know what they want, and they sometimes act differently then what they say.*

Then Joe thinks about the idea brought to him by the head of information technology, Gabrielle. The suggestion is to look at behavioral profiles of the customer base and see which behaviors are most closely linked to churn. In particular, one idea is to look at the relationship between the individual's own call network and churn. It would be something of a social-graph analysis. If they can determine linkages, they may be able modify behavior through appropriate micro-marketing strategies.

Joe is intrigued by this somewhat tactical, but low risk approach...*Why not give it a go?*

Two months later, the results of the pilot are impressive. It turns out that when people drop off the network, the probability of their social contacts also dropping off the network increases dramatically. This is a much stronger predictor than any of the other data the COO has, and even more impressive than that, there is some specificity in what can be done to address the problem. Based on the pilot, micro-marketing tactics are triggered as soon as a particular type of customer drops off the network, and promotional messages including a new phone subsidy or an invoice credit are sent to some or all the people within the churned customer's network. At the end of the comparative study, the rate of churn where these tactics were applied versus the control group is significantly lower. The results are so profound that Joe decides to roll the program out companywide.

Soon, the company churn rates are stabilized, and the company is even beginning to gain back share. Joe sits back in his chair, no longer feeling so embattled. He thinks about how much is being spent on the large loyalty tracking study...

*****

It used to be that the Market Research industry was like the movie *Ground Hog Day* where one wakes up, day after day, and everything is exactly the same as it was the day before. Industry conferences focused on repackaged statistical techniques or data collection, and the untold truth of "what is old is new again" went on for many years. While this conservative approach has provided the industry with consistent single digit growth rates for a long time, it is now a problematic posture. For a traditional Market Research firm whose position is neither strategic nor inexpensive, it is a compromised existence and one very different than the past. This is because there is disruptive change occurring, and for those who sit and wait for the change, the outcome will likely be brutish. For those that embrace the change, and make moves now to capitalize, good fortunes are likely in store.

One foundational issue for the Market Research industry is that the very label of "Market Research" implies a focus on process and data, rather than on decision making. This focus has put the industry into a comfortable state of self-absorption where researchers take pride in their esoteric knowledge about analytical techniques and the pros and cons of various scales. In fact, the definition of Market Research has nothing to do with actual extraction of value or strategic guidance within the organization and the focus on things such as instrument design, data collection, and analytics add no value in-and-of themselves. Certainly, these things are important, but they must be put into the context of the critical business questions for which the information flows. Researchers are often dancing on the head of a pin. The point is missed that if decision makers are not listening to the answer, techniques and scales used in the process really have no meaning.

Corporate executives see Market Research as a stepping stone and young professionals often fall into the function rather than aspiring to it. The perception of Market Research as a back room administrative function is a self-fulfilling prophecy. What's even clearer is that many researchers have happily retreated into this domain, and to their dismay, are then left out of organizational decision making. A typical scenario in the past is where an executive comes to the researcher and asks advice about the direction of the business. The researcher, running from project to project administering research specifications, is woefully unprepared to answer and defensively starts talking about the data itself. This response reinforces the idea that the researcher has no business taking part in management discussions since the researcher is caught up in providing data, not *guidance*. The high ranking manager returns to the executive suite with his original understanding reinforced that the Market Researcher is nothing more than a fact-checker.

This situation is not always the fault of the researcher. The messages that are sent to the research department are often contradictory. The function is told to provide deep thought that can guide the organization to a position of competitive advantage, but at the same time it is told to provide more data, more quickly, and at a lower price point. And while great lip service is paid to the independence of the data, if a high ranking executive has already made a decision based on intuition, then the information provided better agree with his direction or it will likely be attacked. In this dualistic environment, the perception that Market Research is a complex process requiring a certain level of expertise and a 'hands off' approach has allowed research professionals some measure of independence and assurance of data integrity. On the other hand, it has kept the research team in something of an academic vacuum, never traveling too far off campus into the real world.

If executive management is serious about giving the research function a seat at the table, they need to bring the research professional in at the earliest stages of the initiative process. It isn't fair for management to expect instantaneous deep thinking around a business issue to which the researcher previously had no real exposure. The bigger issue for many organizations is that the maturity of their insights function has not progressed from a pure research function to one of true insights and guidance.

*****

The Market Research industry is facing disruptive change and, similar to the changes in media and advertising, the primary driver is technology. In the past, a company would survey people in order to collect attitudinal and behavioral information, and then analyze this data alongside other 'desk research' in order to figure out how to service a customer or decide on what new products to bring to market. While this is still the basic foundation of the Market Insights function, so much demographic, attitudinal, and behavioral data is being collected on-line, and the latest-generation business intelligence (BI) and artificial intelligence (AI) systems are so much better equipped to make sense of it all, that certain survey-based research data is becoming relatively less valuable. The world is pushing in a direction that focuses more on the tangible nature of behavioral analytics and revealed preferences, rather than stated attitudes and behavioral intent. Where there is still a need to collect attitudinal and behavioral-intent data, such as in strategic foresight situations and innovation environments, social-network feeds and on-line communities are providing platforms to efficiently generate this information. The software, often called an Enterprise-Feedback-Management (EFM) system, disrupts another key part of the insights industry which is based on the complexities of data collection. As if these changes were not enough, advances in cognitive science and behavioral economics challenge the contextual underpinnings of the decision making process itself. The changes invite broad questions regarding the specific role of Market Research in the future of the organization, as well as the impact of increasingly large networks of data created from e-commerce transactions, search behavior, and social networks. Indeed, these latter forces are reshaping not only the Market Research function, but the very nature of commerce itself.

Consider the purchase experience of today's buyers who are bombarded by various influence streams increasingly customized with respect to their demographic profile, past behaviors, and stated or implied preferences. As the buyer engages, he or she seamlessly enters a consideration phase and is able to assess the product or service, directly ask questions, consider the opinions of important others, and choose a configuration within budget. The three stages of awareness, consideration, and purchase are blurred as information flows freely back and forth between company and consumer. This empowered, but increasingly overwhelmed buyer now makes a much more informed (though not necessarily better) purchase decision after having established exactly what brand and features they want, and how much they are willing to pay. In essence, the formation of consumer attitudes and the resultant buying behavior has changed as a result of the internet and social media.

These disruptive changes in how people make brand decisions have great implications for the enterprise. For instance, some organizations now rely less on influencing the buyer at the point of sale and place more emphasis on knowing and influencing the customer's frame of reference prior to the point of sale. The 'no negotiation, no hassle' approach from the auto dealership is an example. That is, the skills of the salesperson at the time of transaction are less important than the analytics and insight used to set expectations and know the buyer's wants and needs[3] prior to the sale. For the enterprise, the consumption of mass-marketed brands becomes the expression of the individual's ego and the extension of the consumer's own brand. The internet and social media has inverted the traditional brand communication models and spending on media is becoming much more of a shotgun approach. In many ways, it's the individual at the center of a narcissistic internet culture, which creates the corporate brand identity. People still join certain social clubs and avoid others, drive a particular car, wear particular clothing, and live in a particular city, but now such behavior may be seen as a sign of mass individualism rather than conformist. The Apple brand provides a great example of this paradoxical phenomenon.

---

[3] It's important to make a distinction between strategic sales and transactional sales since we are speaking more in terms of the latter than the former. Generally speaking, transactional sales involve a purchase of a commoditized product that is relatively easy to compare. Strategic sales are more aligned with a complex product or service that is often associated with an ongoing relationship. Some of the characteristics of the strategic sale are smaller volume of customers, larger deal sizes, longer sales cycle, multi-step sales process, and team decision making. An example of a strategic sale is a large consulting engagement in a B2B environment, whereas the classic transactional sale is that of a car or a household appliance.

Affinity with the Apple brand holds the promise of being a unique expression of the individual, but at the same time, it represents entry into the class of the modern-day bourgeoisie.

This unique expression of an individual's brand is publicly advertised through Facebook, and other on-line and off-line channels, and success for the brand is comprised of metrics such as site hits and number and status of on-line friends. In aggregate, these individuals morph into powerful tribes that can often determine the success or failure of the overall corporate brand or particular franchise. Today when a corporation thinks about the influence of *important others* in the brand decision process, they must abide by the fact that consumers will often pay more attention to an aggregate of reviewers on the web, than to traditional mass media, a salesman, or potentially even a spouse or a neighbor.

Given this backdrop, the latest generation of Business Intelligence systems is converging with Market Research to become the organizational lighthouse. Rather than decisions being made on managers' gut feel, evidence-based management guides the organization; and those most familiar with the data and its implications will gain a significant professional edge. These analysts will have the ear of the powerful CFO, CIO, COO, or CMO, and be a critical ally for everyone in the organization. Of course, this new model threatens the traditional Market Research function as behavioral and social network data now regularly encroach onto its territory, and new models of gathering information substitute automated software applications for data collection services (the former bread and butter of the industry).

Information technology, fundamental shifts in how companies look at markets, and attacks on traditional decision theory are serving to disrupt the previously insulated and tranquil Market Research industry. Exploring these foundational shifts and looking at how the industry leaders and companies are dealing with these shifts, is the crux of this book.

*****

Part One of the book looks into three general trends and the impacts of each on the industry. Since technological change underpins two of the three trends discussed, it has been incorporated directly into the topics. The first topic is Big Data and by extension, Business Intelligence systems. Behavioral data is becoming so prolific and predictive modeling is so powerful that the impact of these systems cannot be ignored. The second chapter looks at the impact of the Long Tail and the idea of crowdsourcing. End-user participation in everything from product development to advertising fundamentally changes the world of research. The final chapter in the first section is entitled Situated Cognition. Leading thinkers in the world of decision-making argue that reason and emotion cannot be analyzed in a modular fashion; and this has a critical impact on the collection and use of data.

Part Two of the book shifts to the industry players including the corporate insights department, the insights supplier, and the insights professional. Given the game-changing trends in the industry, individuals as well as companies are struggling with their next move. For the corporation, the emphasis must be on tearing down the walls between information systems and the insights department. Only when the insights department can seamlessly access *all* available data, will the function provide real competitive advantage for the broader organization. The anatomy of such a department as well as the process for getting there is discussed in Chapter Four. For the insights supplier, it is a very challenging time and this is especially true for the strategic partner business model. Upstream entries from management consultancies and information technology consultancies create a more crowded space than ever; but given that this ground defines the future of the organization, it is worth the fight. Beyond those few firms that can establish a trusted advisor relationship in the new order of things, niche software and low-cost service models will also have a space. Each of these models, as well as different go-to-market approaches are discussed, in turn, in Chapter Five. Chapter Six explores the role and critical skill sets of tomorrow's insights professional. Because of the expansive nature of the skillset and the multi-faceted role that tomorrow's insights professional plays in the organization, this person is referred to as an *uberanalyst* throughout the book. Indeed, such an analyst may be as likely to come from the database side of the house as the traditional research department, but what's important is that the person has an interdisciplinary approach to analysis.

Part I: The Changing World of Market Insights

Chapter 1 –Big Data

In the era of big data, more isn't just more. More is different.

- Chris Anderson, Wired Magazine

Tim, the Vice President of Market Research for US Telco, can't quite put it all together. His boss Lucas just told him that his budget may be cut 20% even though revenue and profit are stabilizing. At the same time, he's heard through the grapevine that Gabrielle's IT budget is increasing. Furthermore, she's being consulted on marketing analysis issues which has traditionally been Tim's domain.

Tim calls Sanjit, one of his most trusted Directors, into his office and asks about the analytics that Gabrielle's team is doing. Sanjit tells him about the predictive modeling and the subsequent micro-marketing campaign that was able to stem the churn issue. Tim knew about the effort, but he didn't realize it was going to get this kind of traction. Tim tries to make sense of it all.

The churn work his group has been doing is actually some of the most sophisticated he has ever done. He thinks about how far the analysis has come since the time he spent with a boutique loyalty research firm in Palo Alto in the late-1990s. He recalls a study his firm did in partnership with the consulting firm Hoopers & Lyber that showed a correlation between company revenue and customer satisfaction. He remembers the initial roll-out presentation because he asked if there was a causal relationship. The answer had come back that it was not a causal relationship per se, but there was a strong correlation. He takes pride in knowing that the work his group is doing on the retail study is actually showing a causal relationship. Since US Telco has so much data, they are able to control for just about everything including things like trade area, store volume, and seasonality. It turns out the there is a causal relationship between customer delight and profitability. He knows this is powerful stuff and another example of how Big Data is changing things.

Tim's real challenge is trying to move the needle on customer delight; and this is an entirely different story. Tim thinks to himself… *I finally have real linkage between customer attitude and profitability in the loyalty study, but I still can't seem to do anything about it. It's such a Herculean task to change the customer-service behavior of people in the organization; and that's what it's going to take to improve the customer delight metric. A flip of a switch apparently implemented the micro-marketing campaign that solved much of the churn issue. I know these are really different things and we need to focus on both issues, but how do I compete with those kinds of immediate results? One thing is certain: Predictive models are driving all of this, and I really need to get more involved with these BI tools…*

✱✱✱✱✱

Big Data is one of these terms that means different things to different people. It's generally accepted that Big Data refers to all data that we can put into an on-line environment. This includes the overwhelming amount of demographic, behavioral and attitudinal data that is being produced from consumer-based-on-line activities; it includes massive amounts of off-line data that is being put into an on-line environment; and it includes what is called meta-data, or data about data. When we think of information aggregators such as the US Government, Facebook, Amazon, Google, and others, it's the data created by data, also called data 'exhaust', which is a store of enormous value; and in turn, valuations. Generally speaking, the idea of Big Data includes the notion that the amount of data being considered surpasses our ability to effectively organize, store, and manage it[4]. (For instance, as companies start getting into very large data sets, traditional relational databases have a hard time scaling due to their underlying organization of data and how they access and process the data. Massively-Parallel Processing (MPP) and cloud computing are maturing technologies that promise the ability to harness the power of Big Data.) For the purposes of this book, Big Data can simply be thought of as the deluge of information available to the organization.

In a blue sky sense, Big Data has the potential to change the way the world of discovery works by replacing deductive models with a more exploratory approach. For Market Insights and, more broadly in science, it's been a confirmatory or hypothesis driven approach that has dominated. With Big Data, we can take more inductive approaches to discovery and prediction. That is, instead of formulating a hypothesis on our

---

[4] Footnote: While beyond the scope of this book, the world of business software has consumed much of itself with the challenge of Big Data. Many of the major software companies have invested to take advantage of this expanding market.

own and then testing and revising the hypothesis, the data will present many directions from which we can choose to explore further. Through machine learning and massive data crunching, patterns present themselves to the trained eye (i.e. those with the knowledge of what to look for in the data), and instead of coming up with a potential outcome and trying to figure out the why, we are guided by data patterns and their inherent predictive power to suggest outcomes. Such an approach can be much less laborious than the incremental processes of traditional sciences. The new challenge is that of knowing exactly what to look for in the data.

The Impacts of Big Data on the Market Insights Function:

An Increase in the Importance of the Market Insights Function

The move from a deductive approach to an inductive approach runs parallel to the move from hunch-based management to evidence-based management. In the past, managers who came up with the best story and convinced people of their hypothesis, regardless of what the data said, created action in the organization. More and more, such a situation is being replaced by evidence-based management where decisions are driven by true market information and mere hunches lose their importance. Given this trend, the well positioned Market Insights function becomes the brain of the organization.

As we achieve truly integrated data sets and there is an ability to look at systems both internally and externally in a coherent fashion, executives are provided with one sheet of music and competing scores are dismissed. The time spent arguing about which data is correct, is instead used to process the information and make better business decisions. As this occurs, the basis of management decision-making changes from 80% gut feel and 20% information, to 80% information and 20% gut feel. In this context, information becomes the new currency, and as long as the Market Insights function positions itself as the information synthesizer and puts itself at the center of the information tools being used, its value will rise accordingly.

A Cannibalization of some Primary Quantitative Research

As multiple data sources are integrated across silos in the organization and analysis tools become more sophisticated, the substituting of certain primary research data with Big Data will become more pronounced. Take Google's Price Index (GPI) as an example. The GPI is data exhaust that is ready for Google at the touch of a button. In contrast, the Federal Reserve must literally go out into the real world and collect prices on a city-by-city, store-by-store, and item-by-item basis, to provide the Consumer Price Index (CPI). Another example is connected to the fundamental movement into digital media marketing. As expenditures move away from traditional vertical channels and digital media becomes a greater part of the portfolio, behavior-based analytics become the gold standard for projecting campaign success. Comscore's web analytics or Google's' powerful toolset married with panel-based tracking can measure and predict the success of advertising campaigns and other marketing expenditures across various platforms. There are plenty of other examples where Big Data can act as a 'close enough' surrogate for expensive primary research. One well known uberanalyst sites an example of where the Department of Health and Human Services could get certain statistics from already existing government records rather than commissioning a multi-million dollar survey research project. Other such opportunities start to multiply quickly as Big Data increases.

Especially pertinent to the Market Research industry are trends around social network data, a subset of Big Data. Suppliers are already marketing such data as an alternative to expensive research studies and corporations are testing the waters. Recent examples in the news include a Consumer Packaged Goods (CPG) company including the most popular on-line recipes to help forecast their sales and an automotive company formally tracking customer satisfaction through aggregate on-line consumer sentiment. Such activity is becoming more prominent as companies gain market advantage by combining social media data with the power of web crawling, and artificial intelligence to collect and analyze consumer feedback. Detractors suggest that social networking data is, by its nature, contextually-based information and until we improve the machine's ability to frame, filter, and interpret semantic content, there are still underlying data integrity concerns[5]. While IBM's Watson may have won on Jeopardy, our computer overlord cannot yet fully frame the discussion nor comprehend the contextual complexity of human

---

[5] Footnote: See Sidebar discussion <u>Web Scraping and Sources of Error.</u>

sentiment. That said, the speed and cost factors of social media analysis are just right for many of today's organizations.

Sidebar Discussion: **Web Scraping and Sources of Error**

There is a lot of attention being paid to social media and the opinion information that is produced through web scraping tools (a.k.a. contextual inquiry tools, etc.) While it is hard to argue with the qualitative information produced and the contextual value it provides, the quantitative value of such data is still suspect. Myriad supplier-companies are putting together social media offerings that do everything from forecasting sales to measuring brand equity, but they are having a difficult time convincing the information-savvy corporation. The challenge is that the data suffers from critical sources of error.

For example, **Non-response error** *is an issue for social media data. We might think of non-response as the silent majority of those on the internet whom are only passive participants in social media. Similarly,* **coverage error** *is* *something to be concerned about when discussing social media data. While there certainly may be a high percentage of the Internet Generation on-line, people in under developed countries and elderly people are prime examples of underrepresented populations. For this reason, social-media data may be much less relevant for a car targeted at baby boomers than one targeted at the Internet Generation. Finally, <u>measurement error</u> is an area of concern when analyzing social media data. There is no structured approach to how the data is collected (i.e. no common instrument), and a herd mentality exists in every corner of the social media universe (i.e. no true sample independence); thus, in some ways, it is hard to objectively assess such information separately from the marketing function itself.*

A Move towards Data-Driven Storytelling

Given the overwhelming amount of information and the competition for attention in today's organization, insights managers need to care as much about the story itself as they do about things like statistical significance or the integrity of the data collection methodology. It isn't to say that the soundness of the data is not important, but it's quickly turning into table-stakes and is only important in as much as there is a level of trust of the data quality[6]. That is, the data must be a high enough quality that it is defensible if attacked, but it's the data-driven story that creates a compelling case that drives action in the organization. And action is the reason business research is commissioned.

An Increase in Mixed Methodology Research

As focus shifts from data collection to storytelling and higher quality insights, the multiple sources of information available is leading to mixed methodological approaches. That is, information converges to answer the specific business question. A study that artfully and scientifically marries internal and external databases, web listening, and a mixed-mode 'quali-quant' approach may be seen as the gold standard for an important initiative.

An Emergence of Information-Integration-And-Quality-Control Departments

Mixed methodology research brings a new set of challenges. As multiple tributaries flow into the larger river of information, several questions arise such as the underlying pollution level of the water (i.e. information quality) and how the tributaries should be damned (i.e. how information should be weighted.) As the number and sources of information increase, quality control and the processes that surround

---

[6] Footnote: See section below: *An emergence of information-integration-and-quality-control departments.*

information integration will likely become its own domain. That is, an information-integration-and-quality-control function will likely emerge in some organizations; and certain supplier firms will come in to fill this niche. In this department, technology and research expertise will again converge.

An Increase in Some Types of Qualitative Research

Alongside of the storytelling trend, there is an increasing appetite for deep-dive qualitative methods that provide in-depth attitudinal profiles of interesting markets and segments. While data itself can be dull and often easily ignored, deep dive qualitative research can tell a great story and communicate significant customer understanding. There are a number of different techniques and none of them need take place in traditional focus group facilities. Ethnography, where someone is observed in their natural environment, is becoming more important, as are projective techniques and other creative ways to elicit ideas[7]. On-line bulletin boards where teams of people help develop ideas in an iterative and immersive format is as adaptation of yesterday's face-to-face Delphi methods. As mobile and other technologies progress, other traditional methods such as diary research are moving on-line with subjects providing mobile video diaries. All of these deep-dive techniques can be used to bring to life ideas and thoughts that would otherwise remain latent in the market.

Of course, the outcome is just as important as the techniques themselves and this is where deep-dive qualitative

---

[7] Also see the discussion of ideation and metaphor elicitation trends in the following chapter.

research can really shine. From the pain a healthcare patient feels as they try to navigate the complexities of the health care system, to the emotions of a new mother wrestling with the needs of a new born baby, customer perspective is brought to life in different and exciting ways.

A Decrease in Others Types of Qualitative Research

Web listening is replacing some of the exploratory qualitative research on the front-end of projects and some of the contextual qualitative research on the back-end of projects. Before web listening became the norm, a company might use a focus group or a series of focus groups to determine specific questions to ask on a quantitative study or to determine specific answer lists. Similarly, on the back-end of a project, groups or follow-up executive interviews were once more commonly used to further explore the quantitative research outcomes, add color to the study's conclusions, or to sort through recommendations. While these techniques are still of use in certain circumstances, social media can often provide the necessary information without commissioning additional qualitative research.

An Increase in Info Graphics, Data Visualization, and Videography

In parallel with the rise in data driven storytelling, info graphics and data visualization are becoming a much more important part of the insights function. Managers lament the uselessness of endless reams of data and instead look to represent entire bodies of integrated knowledge through visual representation. The story will need to come to life in order for the message to be heard above the other noise in the organization. Much like in the advertising and messaging world, data analytics and Market Insights will come to depend more on the concepts of visualizing and storyboarding their big ideas. If a picture is worth a thousand words, then a knowledge-driven graphic or a video example of the big idea must be worth a million static bars of data.

Chapter 2- The Long Tail

> About the time we can make the ends meet, somebody moves the ends.
>
> - Herbert Hoover

Tim sits at his desk and considers how he will cut his budget. The best place to start is probably the big relationship tracking studies. Altogether, they are costing him over ten million dollars. He has three major relationship tracking surveys: a brand tracking and competitor benchmarking study, a loyalty tracking study, and a retail tracking study. Tim knows the loyalty study, in particular, should be revisited since he hasn't bid it out in a number of years. Furthermore, he may be able to somehow consolidate the different studies under one umbrella and gain some economies of scale. Tim looks at an article on his desk talking about the power of the new EFM platforms that are now in the market. The article talks about how sample is becoming ubiquitous and crowdsourcing through communities is becoming a best practice for the industry. It promises to save a lot of money. He also notices that there are a lot more suppliers calling him regarding these types of communities and EFM solutions.

Tim thinks about the changes in data collection methodologies over the years. He chuckles when he thinks about how much they have changed. When he first came into the field of research in the mid-1990s, the Internet was still so new. Surveys were still almost exclusively done by phone and mail. Where computers were used, physical disks were sent out for people to give their responses. Since it was a client-server environment, it was impossible to do it the way it is done today. It wasn't until the late 90s that the first nth tier architecture came into the market and surveys were able to be done over the Internet. Email survey invitations have been dominant ever since, but now there's another shift going on.

Tim thinks about his customer base. *We're still collecting data almost exclusively by e-mail, but a lot of our base, especially the younger generation, may not even be looking at their email anymore. They are using social platforms and texting probably even more than e-mail. Communities are what everyone is talking about and we need to get on board.* He makes a mental note to call a couple of the suppliers that have been leaving him messages...

*****

The Long Tail is an idea popularized by a book written by Chris Anderson from Wired Magazine. In statistical terms, the *Long Tail* refers to the idea that the larger share of population rests within the tail of a probability distribution. In marketing terms, the concept of the Long Tail essentially extends the Pareto principle (i.e. the idea that the majority of the market is dominated by the minority of the customers) by suggesting that the lion's share of a market is now dominated by the many rather than the few. In many ways, the concept of the Long Tail can be thought of as the democratization of commerce (much like the globalization trend).

Driven by the ubiquity and power of the internet, the Long Tail is fundamentally changing business strategy and communications. At a foundational level, company success becomes a function of the ability to customize, market, and distribute their products to a much wider and a much more heterogeneous cohort of people[8]. Micro-marketing replaces mass customization. Mass media and traditional advertising models are disrupted as vertical communication strategies give way to grass roots and digitally based marketing techniques.

A classic example of the Long Tail phenomenon is Amazon.com in the on-line book market. This on-line retailer is able to create new markets, not only because it has access to markets (i.e. almost universal awareness and distribution through the web), but because it is able to source customized product. In lock-step with changes in the publishing industry, it is able to marry micro-marketing and distribution with micro-publishing; thereby impacting both the supply and demand sides of the equation.

The Long Tail extends itself into the Market Insights in multiple ways, but most importantly through *crowdsourcing*. With so many folks available and willing to give feedback on

---

[8] Footnote: The direction of some CPG companies is actually to reduce their Stock-keeping units (SKU) and it may be argued that this direction is opposite of moving towards a micro-marketing strategy. These companies are looking to reduce the choice environment and still cover the vast majority of their customer's needs. For example, the company may see that 60% of their SKUs provide for virtually 90% of customer needs, and act accordingly. Other CPG companies continue in the direction of customizing to micro-market needs and are expanding their SKUs. While only time will tell which approach is a better one, the different strategies do reveal that the brick-and-mortar-retail environment should be considered separately when thinking about the phenomenon of the Long Tail.

new markets, products and ideas, the Long Tail gives a new and increasingly important channel for the Voice of the Customer (VOC).

The Impacts of the Long Tail on the Market Insights Function:

A Commoditization of Some Data Collection and a Move to Research Communities

Much in the same way that e-mail revolutionized the way survey data was collected in the late 1990s, on-line communities, interactive software, mobile technology, and the ease of acquiring sample over the internet, are combining to change the world of research once again. Where lengthy questionnaires with their massive matrices and repetitive questioning would drive survey fatigue and abandonment, crowdsourcing tools and interactive technologies (e.g. research through gaming) are quickly becoming the preferred method of collecting market feedback[9]. While companies such as Facebook have yet to truly monetize the field of data collection [10], on-line tools companies and web listening software allow for easy qualitative and quantitative data collection. This trend is empowering corporate purchasing

---

[9] Footnote: This section does not refer to revealed preference and behavioral data collection methods (e.g. scanner panel data, EEG data, NFC data, geo-market data, etc.) which are providing differentiation for companies; but rather survey data-collection.

[10] Footnote: As of this writing, LinkedIn is beginning to sell its ability to target micro-segments based on their business network information.

departments in the acquisition of research services and encouraging some companies to manage their own panels and their own research initiatives. Some leading companies are starting to look outside only for software tools or very narrow domains of expertise.

One way for the insights manager to think about these emerging software tools and on-line communities is in terms of quantitative and qualitative platforms [11]. The qualitative platform allows for small branded relationship-building forums and provides a more intimate setting for different types of community feedback. These groups are carefully configured within particular affinity groups in order to build trust of participants and a higher sense of involvement. These qualitative forums are often ad hoc in nature and often aligned with a particular marketing campaign (or brand franchise) where participants may be tapped from early innovation phases through message creation and in a more limited sense, market validation.

A legitimate quantitative platform has a wider membership and acts more like a traditional proprietary panel, but there are some key differences from the traditional vendor-driven

---

[11] Some may argue that the quantitative community platform is more like a traditional proprietary panel and an on-line community suggests more of a qualitative approach, but these lines are blurring. The only real difference is the community engagement approach is the nature of the application itself. Some platforms are built for qualitative needs and others are built to address quantitative needs. Due to tradeoffs in the software development these are generally different applications, but they may be combined and may both be considered research communities.

approach. The ease of acquiring sample, ease of use, interactive nature, and the ability to present quantitative results back to stakeholders in a visually interesting manner allows the corporation to build their own *panel communities* with minimal hand holding. As has always been the case, the engaged user is much more apt to give feedback and provide critical insights; and since the tool complexity is being removed, companies are capitalizing on the opportunity to bring such do-it-yourself (DIY) tools in house.

There are a couple of important implications of this commoditization trend. First, the emergence of research communities starts to bridge the divide between the marketer and the research itself; and crowdsourcing becomes an integrated part of both the product development and marketing lifecycle. The second related outcome is that the crowdsourcing platform tools become integrated with organizational systems. If this is not done, these toolsets will likely become the domain of the technology consulting firm, the digital marketing firms, media firms or the more progressive research firms.

Sidebar Discussion: **The Democratization of Survey Research and the Guerilla Marketer**

Marketers are increasingly using survey research as a tool of influence. Instead of making an unsubstantiated claim regarding a product, service, or government policy, they may hire or set up their own third-party entity to do a survey and create the impression of objectivity. While this ethically-questionable approach has always been used to some degree in the field of survey research and opinion polls, the democratization of surveys combined with new media communication structures (i.e. the grass-roots nature of the internet versus the vertical structure of traditional mass media) makes the tactic much easier to carry out.

A Movement of Innovation Research from the Domain of the Few to the Domain of the Many

Innovation research will increase due to the Long Tail phenomenon and globalization trends. More niche markets are created and these markets provide demand for many different products and offers. One of the challenges for the corporation will be getting a good read on the true potential of these new markets. This will drive more money into innovation research such as deep dive qualitative research and foundational market structure studies like segmentation, market sizing, and brand positioning.

Besides increasing the need for innovation research, the Long Tail changes the nature of the research itself. The participation of the Long Tail has moved user innovation from the domain of the few to the domain of the many. It used to be that innovation research would be been done in a unilateral fashion with a small group of influential customers as part of the research and development (R&D) process, but that is changing with the participation of the Long Tail and the willingness of the marketplace to both generate and refine ideas.

In the case of the software industry, it has always been the norm for new technology to be vetted in the marketplace. Once software is released, the marketplace provides feedback that drives bug fixes as well as new features and functionality. Today, with web-based communities and innovation forums, this ability to leverage the know-how and insights of an entire population of end-users, is spread to multiple industries. These users, especially those in high involvement categories from automobiles to smartphones, are excited to share ideas to create and refine products and services. Likely, as interactive technology tools get better, such user-based innovation models will become more prominent.

A Fragmentation of Advertising Research

The phenomenon of the Long Tail is also changing advertising research in fundamental ways. Digital media and multi-channel content distribution models are driving a need for entirely new measurement systems. When the industry only had a few channels to measure (television, radio, and print, etc.) and it was clear which companies controlled those channels, it was relatively straightforward to gather information and provide measurements. Today, everyone seems to be developing their own content and there are myriad distribution channels. As a result, measuring return on marketing investment across the portfolio is becoming a more complex task. Models that have acted as currency in the media buying world are being challenged and industry standard measurement systems are no longer 100% agreed upon. Panel-based web tracking, being advanced by companies such as Comscore, highlight not only this particular challenge, but also the challenge to tracking internet behavior based solely on cookies that can be deleted off a user's computer (i.e. such an approach potentially overstates numbers).

Copy testing is also changing. It used to be that an advertising firm would create a campaign, test the copy, make refinements, and then launch. The campaign was usually a single concept and somewhat complete before it was tested and sent out to market. As with innovation research, a unilateral model prevailed. Today, instead of testing a fully-baked advertising concept, a digital marketing firm may present less of a complete idea and more of a seed concept. The key is that the firm has the ability to present multiple concepts through multiple channels, in multiple markets and get not only validation on the concepts it should pursue, but ideas on how to take those ideas to the next level. It looks more like a concept screening initiative where many ideas are reduced to a few winners. This crowdsourcing process allows users to vet the best campaigns without lengthy copy testing research and it creates an interactive feedback loop for input into the next creative phase. An agency may now take 20 concepts (instead of one) and conduct an iterative process of feedback and development whereby it abandons some ideas and develops others. While some may argue that methods such as internet based dial-testing have been done for years in copy testing, today's interactive measurement environments are more advanced and the formation of the Long Tail means that number of available participants have increased dramatically. Furthermore, crowdsourcing and streamlined-software approaches to copy testing take the time to test from multiple weeks to a few days.

A Move to Behavioral Clustering in Segmentation Research

Companies conduct elaborate segmentation studies with large qualitative and quantitative research components. The approach is to collect data and artfully cluster segments into a manageable few that are presumed to be homogeneous. Once this is complete, the company needs to find those segments; an entirely different challenge. The Long Tail fundamentally disrupts this old approach of needs-based or attitudinal segmentation, as the relative homogeneity assumption in the market becomes more questionable. The problem is that our markets are becoming less homogeneous and this idea of mass customization is giving way to more of a niche marketing environment. Audiences are smaller, more autonomous, and more self-defined. At the same time, predictive analytics and Big Data can allow us to not only look at behavioral data to more accurately predict these niche segments, but more importantly, to act upon the data and better attach ROI to our strategies. It's not to say that we should never conduct attitudinal or stated-needs-based segmentation, but if it was difficult to define, find, and market to these segments before, it is doubly hard to do so now.

Chapter 3- Situated Cognition

Tim looks at the books on his shelf and pulls down the book, Influence, by Robert Cialdini. It's been one of his favorite marketing books ever since he read it in business school. It talks about how people make decisions and how irrational they behave when doing so. According to the book, reason has very little to do with how people act; instead we're pre-programmed and free-will is something of a misnomer. Affinity, social proof, consistency, authority, liking, reciprocity, scarcity; these are the things that elicit the powerful "click, wrrrrrrrrrrrrrr" response in our brain. The anecdotes and the research are powerful and it just makes sense to Tim. He thinks about all the decision making models he's seen through the years and assumptions that feed them. Perhaps he needs to buy a copy of Influence for a few of his suppliers...

* * * * *

Situated Cognition or grounded cognition is the idea that cognition cannot be separated from the real world context in which the thinking takes place. For instance, the person in a cold room is more inclined to answer a question negatively than the person in a warm room. In fact, all of our senses spill over into cognitive evaluations and it is therefore impossible to study things such as emotions and reason in a modular fashion. Likely, a better distinction is unconscious and conscious decision making; where the unconscious mind takes into account all of our environmental associations and actually has the ability to override our conscious evaluations. At its root, modern cognitive scientists[12] have shifted the discussion from one in which people have conceptual knowledge and apply these concepts to make sense of a situation, to one in which the person's immediate situation (including feelings derived from environment, people, and culture) determines the cognitive evaluation.

The Impacts of Situated Cognition on the Market Insights Function:

A Shift in Economic Schools of Thought

The shifts in cognitive science run parallel to many of the changes in economic thought including a move away from neo-classical thought towards behavioral economics. The neo-classical approach has dominated economics and traditional Market Research for a very long time. The neo-classical approach postulates that individuals are rational actors, or in micro-economic terms, they are *optimizers*. This implies that

---

[12] Footnote: The ideas of cognitive science in this chapter may be attributed to Antonio Damasio (University of Southern California), Gerald Zaltman (Harvard University), and Norbert Schwartz (University of Michigan).

people approach decisions by using only their reasoning abilities to evaluate the pros and cons of the decision, and then act accordingly.

More modern theory, such as behavioral economics, suggests that while reasoned evaluations do play an important role, affective behavior is just as important, if not more important. For instance, if you are feeling particularly fearful, this emotion may fog your rational judgment and make you behave in an irrational way. Furthermore, in uncertain choice environments, individuals are more likely to consider only surface information by using a heuristic mechanism (a subjective lens that helps categorize things) and not truly optimize their choices. This experiential lens allows the decider to make a good enough decision when the entirety of information is impossible to process for some reason. According to modern theory, individuals are not *optimizers* working with perfect information, but rather *satisficers* who make rules-based decisions grounded in imperfect information.

A Greater Focus on Heuristic Drivers of Behavior

The idea of the individual as a *satisficer* who uses heuristics to make decisions will start to dominate decision making models. Ideas such as Herbert Simon's *bounded rationality*[13] are gaining renewed prominence while models that rely solely on optimal choice behavior are declining. More focus is placed on intangible attributes of the brand such as trust and affinity

---

[13] Footnote: The idea of *bounded rationality* is that people are bounded by the information they have to make a decision, the time they have to make a decision, and by their cognitive ability to make a decision.

and a decreasing emphasis is placed on studying tangible factors such as features and functionality.

An Emphasis on Revealed Preference over Stated Preference

The insights function is placing much more weight on behavioral data and actual trends in the market rather than relying on stated behavioral intent analyzed through survey data. This makes particular sense in light of the advances in the cognitive sciences and our knowledge that the unconscious impacts on a decision at one moment may be very different than those at another moment. It is very difficult to build good models based on stated preference and stated intent if the main decision drivers of that preference are not stable[14].

An Increased Interest in Experiential Market Research

Nuero-marketing research, eye tracking research, and even research based on how your stomach is acting when you make a decision have come and (to some degree) gone as mainstream topics in Market Insights. The desire for this type of research is understandable as it looks more at actual physiological factors of decision making and therefore seems to align more with revealed behavior and the newer schools of behavioral thought.

---

[14] Footnote: This trend does not necessarily suggest a decline in primary research. In fact, experiential research and research involving contextual consumer decision is increasing. Even if imperfect, there is still a great appetite for forward looking information especially in untapped and fast paced markets.

The challenge is that this research is often times expensive, complex, and it's very difficult to tie to a particular ROI. For instance, it's easy to see that a particular area of the brain is engaged when one makes a decision about a brand, but the interpretation by the analyst may obscure the facts. Imagine a particular ad registering more of a reaction than another. This may show us that it is good creative and it grabs a viewer's attention, but it really tells us nothing about *breakthrough* and the associate brand promise. It does not give the researcher much in terms of deciding on a particular message beyond a few attention grabbing words.

As the body of work reaches a critical mass, the research will likely yield more practical results. Foundational case studies allowing companies to compare successful campaigns with very specific physiological activity will likely bring the work into the main-stream. Today, it is still in an early adopter phase; being developed in very large companies and academic environments.

An Increase in Attention Paid to Implicit Bias in Data

Implicit bias is introduced when the unconscious mind or perception of the situation influences our evaluation. An example of implicit bias: if a man has long hair, you may subconsciously associate him with the creative field rather than, say, the world of finance. Different cultures and different age groups will have different implicit bias that will also impact their evaluations. Such bias has important implications for primary research and instrument design. For instance, question order and response order should be carefully considered in light of the target audience. The fact that a Chinese consumer will have a different implicit bias than an American consumer should impact both design and interpretation.

An Increase in the Use of Conceptual Metaphor in Brand Research

Conceptual metaphor refers to the understanding of one idea, or conceptual domain in terms of another. Such metaphors are seen in everyday life and shape the way we think and interpret the world around us. For example, the idea of the 'road ahead' suggests that we are travelling through time and that such a journey may come with 'bumps', or painful experiences in life. Such metaphors are becoming more and more prominent to elicit ideas that cannot be readily articulated (e.g. the next iPhone). The power resides in such metaphors to uncover latent needs in the marketplace as well as communication strategies targeting the unconscious mind. This is especially useful in areas such as brand innovation and communications.

Part II: A Roadmap for the 21st Century

Chapter 4- The Corporate Insights Function

> Most discussions of decision making assume that only senior executives make decisions or that only senior executives' decisions matter. This is a dangerous mistake.
> - **Peter Drucker**

Tim considers how he might overcome the current situation. Certainly the new Business Intelligence tools are here to stay and it looks like Gabrielle's people are starting to take the lead. He figures that, at a minimum, he needs to set up liaisons between his group and Gabrielle's group. He needs to make sure people are being trained on the new business intelligence tools and that it is his team that is presenting the information to marketing and management. In order to do this, he will approach Gabrielle to partner more closely with her. Tim team's highly trained statisticians and analysts should really be involved with driving these solutions and Gabrielle's knowledge of what's going on with this new class of tools will help him make sense of everything. Furthermore, when he evaluates suppliers, he's going to make sure the people he brings in know a thing or two about Big Data.

Tim thinks to himself, *I've always liked Gabrielle. It'll be a good alliance...*

*****

In today's corporation, the role and value of Market Research is often questioned when data is collected and analyzed without solid business context. Herein is a key difference between traditional Market Research and Market Insights; Market Insights takes into account the entire body of available information while Market Research often ignores any information beyond the purview of a particular unified methodology.

Recent years have seen the rise in titles such as "insights and analytics" attached to the Market Research function in order to enhance and refocus the role of these groups. In other organizations, traditional Market Research departments are being completely consumed into other business units because the value of a stand-alone Market Research function is not apparent to upper management. In order avoid such a fate, the insights team must start by understanding the basic anatomy of what makes an insights department, where they are in terms of a baseline, and how to most effectively achieve the status of a trusted advisory team.

Understanding the Anatomy of a Successful Insights Function

Figure 1: The Three Rings of a Successful Insights Function

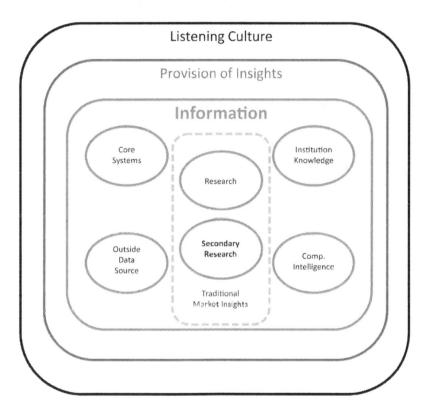

The solid inner ring of Figure 1, entitled Information Sources, encompasses all available information within the organization. The inside dotted line represents the more traditional Market Research function whose charter is to conduct primary research and acquire secondary Market

Research data. The third major source of information, represented by the upper left hand circle, revolves around the internal enterprise systems that track things like finance and billing, customer marketing databases, and operational systems (i.e. the company's traditional ERP and CRM systems). The lower left hand circle represents external data provided by organizations such as Google, the US Government; or the massive amounts of data provided by web scraping. The lower right circle represents competitive intelligence which gets into much of the companies benchmarking protocols. Finally, and perhaps most importantly, there's the institutional knowledge that may not be captured in the other knowledge areas. This institutional knowledge will often be the most important since it can speak to what's been tried in the past and the organizational politics surrounding particular decisions. This institutional knowledge can be anything from an executive's team vision, to competitive insights dormant in the sales force.

The second solid ring represents the extraction of true insights, or wisdom, from the inner ring of information sources. The provision of insights is really the domain of the insights analyst. Since there are myriad information sources, someone who is skilled at looking at multiple sources of data and putting it into a coherent story is critical to the organization.[15]

Ultimately, the best insights in the world are worthless if nobody is listening. The outer ring represents a continuous advancement of the company's willingness to listen to the

---

[15] Footnote: A discussion of the uberanalyst and the respective skillsets is addressed in more detail in Chapter 6- The Insights Professional.

Market Insights. This is something that starts at the top of the organization and must be culturally engrained across all departments. At the same time, it is the responsibility of the successful insights department to promote such a culture by providing market advantage through their insights, and making sure those at the top of the organization have bought into the insights culture.

Understanding the Levels of Departmental Maturity

Depending on the organization, the insights department will generally be advancing through, or moving back through, one of the following three stages. These stages, in increasing order of maturity, are a *commodity supplier* to the marketing or purchasing department, a respected *decision support team,* or at its highest level, a *trusted advisory team.* Given that the three stages represent a continuum, many departments may in fact be present in two stages simultaneously.

Stage One- Commodity Supplier

Though the insights function is an internal department in this first scenario, the *Commodity Supplier* is more of an order-taker than a true part of the company's fabric. Often reporting to the marketing department, the function is led by a mid-level manager (but in some cases as high as the Vice-President level or the Senior-Vice-President level). Some organizations, unfortunately, are receding into this stage as cost pressures or perception of low-value Market Research has engulfed their thinking.

Evidence that a department is in Stage One is a subordinate relationship with marketing and likely a subordinate relationship with the purchasing department as well. There is no true executive sponsorship and for this reason decisions are often governed by cost control measures. The research staff is usually less experienced in research methodology and lower paid relative to industry average. The staff is usually compensated on a fixed salary basis with a very low portion of the compensation, if any, based on performance. The group as a whole has a lower headcount and a lower budget than its industry peers in Stage Two or Stage Three. This creates an environment that lacks support and managers are usually stretched between many projects. There is really no budget authority emanating from this group given that they have no real management support. In fact, they are generally the last to know about new initiatives or departmental cuts since they do not take part in regular stakeholder meetings. If they are invited to important meetings, it is usually on the tail end of the initiative process.

The result is that research is conducted by the numbers and specifications are written with little or no input from the actual business decision makers. The research is usually tactically focused and low-value questions are asked of the market; whereas high-value questions leading to game changing insights are only peripherally addressed or left out all-together. The findings are written simply as a recasting of what is found in data tabulation tables without any synthesis of information or value-added industry insight. In the silo of the Stage One department, true findings are rare, and truly useful recommendations are practically non-existent.

Stage Two- Decision Support Team

In Stage Two of departmental maturity, the insights team turns into a D*ecision Support Team* and begins to garner more confidence and respect. At this stage, key executive sponsors for the insights function have arrived on the scene, and suddenly people are much more interested in information-based decision making. In this environment, the insights department becomes needed, though not always wanted.[16]

Sidebar Discussion: **The Hidden Agenda**

Many business managers at this stage of organizational maturity (i.e. Stage Two) may just be playing along with the idea of information-based decision making, but really have a hidden agenda not based on market information. These may be savvy high-ranking company executives that espouse the virtues of market insights, but in actuality, they make their decisions based on gut feel and then look for information to support what they've already decided.

(Continued on following page...)

---

[16] Footnote: See Sidebar Discussion: The Hidden Agenda

If the insights department findings and recommendations do not agree with their own assumptions about the market, the executive may begin to casually undermine the legitimacy of the research by pointing out low sample sizes or other possible design weaknesses. It is important for the insights owner to be aware of this agenda and be prepared to either fiercely defend the research recommendations in public, or ideally, find some sort of private diplomatic middle ground with the specific manager that neither compromises the true voice of the market nor results in the executive attacking the study.

Evidence that suggests the insights department is in Stage Two is that the group is seen more as a peer to other functional groups such as marketing, purchasing, IT or operations. At this level, the insights managers are more credible and a bit more seasoned. They may have line management experience and they are likely well versed in either information analysis or in the industry in which the company resides. Sometimes they are versed in both, which makes them more valuable. Importantly, the insights staff is better compensated and often has a portion of compensation tied to performance (as evaluated by internal stakeholders and management). While headcount may or may not be expanded from stage one, it is generally adequate. Unlike a Stage One organization, the group has input into budgets and supplier choice is not driven by 'cost only' considerations. (See Sidebar Discussion – *The Supplier Decision*)

Sidebar Discussion: **The Supplier Decision**

From a Stage One insights department perspective, or similarly, from a purchasing department perspective, all suppliers look alike as long as they say they can meet the specifications on the RFP document. The challenge for the insights team is readily apparent when the supplier does not deliver seamless fielding, value-added analytics or promised report writing expertise. The internal corporate department quickly finds itself overwhelmed troubleshooting issues, and quality insights are often the last thing to garner serious attention.

(Continued on following page...)

> *The Stage Two insights department, on the other hand, has learned from such experiences and is savvy enough to understand and demand a particular level of service in the RFP. A Stage Three organization has a trusted network of supplier advisors who perform in a consistent and high quality manner. While there may be a slight premium associated with the levels of service, there is a fair exchange of value that underlies the trust relationship between partners.*

From an output perspective, the portfolio of studies in the Stage Two department tends to be less tactically focused and more strategically focused[17]. By virtue of being included earlier in the process and having direct access to the business team decisions, the insights team produces demonstrably good reports where most, if not all, of the important business questions are answered. Information is synthesized with previous research and internal sources, and the insights are put into an industry perspective. Recommendations are still primarily the domain of the business manager, but the insights manager provides enlightened perspective for that decision.

---

[17] More brand positioning, market mix, market structure, portfolio analysis, etc. (Also see, Chapter 6, Figure 5, <u>Layers of Insights</u>)

Stage Three- Trusted Advisory Team

The third stage of maturity, the *Trusted Advisory Team*, provides foundational guidance for the organization. At this stage, the CEO and the executive staff have completely bought into the value of the insights function and information-driven decision making. This vision, in turn, permeates the organization. The Market Insights function has become a driving force in the company culture and a source of competitive advantage in the marketplace.

Evidence that suggests the company has achieved Stage Three status is, for example, the value of the function being mentioned in the annual report and shareholder meetings. The CEO and other executives begin to set corporate mission, objectives, and policy based on Market Insights. In Stage Three, Business Intelligence and Market Insights become somewhat interchangeable with a subtle distinction. The insights department passes things through purchasing as a mere formality and sits in stature with teams such as finance or marketing. The powerful C-level managers now see the leaders of the insights function as necessary allies within their ranks.

In Stage Three, the insights managers are well-compensated, performance-driven, and top-tier analysts. These individuals are trained in the science of data analysis and the art of storytelling; they know the organization and the players, and they likely have a certain gravitas about them. Indeed, these insights managers are the uberanalysts to whom we refer throughout the book. Formal processes are in place throughout the organization so that the insights managers are a part of each important meeting during the initiative process, and they are seen as a trusted advisor for each level of the organization. The group as a whole stems from the profile of these individuals, and the function is seen more as an investment center rather than as a cost center. Resources are easier to come by and budget requirements are virtually always met.

The resulting research portfolio is heavily weighted to strategic issues and considerations. While there is tactical research being conducted, it is always as outflow from strategic initiatives. All the right questions are asked of the internal databases and of the customers directly. In fact, the questions themselves are at the very heart of the corporate strategy. Information and insight is grounded in multiple organizational sources and reports are never presented as reams of data with self-evident captions. Rather strategic guidance is rendered on things such as opening new markets, increasing current share of customer wallet, or increasing margin through differentiation. For the Stage Three insights function, the voice of the market acts as a lighthouse for organizational strategy.

Figure 2: 3 Stage Maturity Model

	Stage 1: Commodity Supplier	Stage 2: Decision Support Team	Stage 3: Strategic Advisory Team
Role within Company	Order taker relationship with other divisions Little or no executive support Cost center Not part of the decision team / backroom function	Peer relationship with other divisions Executive sponsorship Strategic cost center Part of decision team	Trusted advisor relationship with other divisions Executive team membership Investment center Critical part of the decision team
Character-istics	Little or no autonomous budget Purchasing and BUs drive decisions	Autonomous funding, but also 'tin can' funding Managers are paid at or above industry average	Autonomous strategy and analytics budget Strategic relationships with internal BUs and external suppliers

	Stage 1: Commodity Supplier	Stage 2: Decision Support Team	Stage 3: Strategic Advisory Team
Character-istics	Often commissions 'low bid' supplier Little cross functional collaboration Managers are paid below industry averages Reports have little if any insights (i.e. 'data dumping')	Expanded headcount over Stage One department Analysts produce insights, but not recommendations	Well compensated staff of uberanalysts Reports seamlessly integrate myriad data sources; findings and recommendations are presented in an engaging manner

Organizing for Success

From a process perspective, the organizational structure defines how teams interact in a cross-functional manner and how insights managers interface with the rest of the organization. This structure is critical to providing competitive advantage to the organization. Depending on things such as size and culture, a number of approaches may be deployed; each with its own trade-offs. The smaller the company, the more likely the insights function is housed centrally or simply engrained in some manner across the operations or marketing fabric of the organization. In a large organization, there may be insights managers embedded in the business units, insights managers supporting just corporate strategy initiatives, and an entire central insights staff that supports companywide initiatives. The different approaches and their respective trade-offs are outlined below.

No matter the specific structure, however, there are three organizing principles that should be observed if the company aspires to Market Insights excellence. *First*, there must be a specific vernacular for market insights that transcends all departments of the organization. If everyone is speaking in different languages, it creates a modern day *Tower of Babel*. The insights function must be organized in a manner that enables it to create uniform standards for designing, communicating and acting upon critical market measurement. *Second*, there needs to be a system that assures data quality and integrates data in a way that attaches value to the source. To use the river analogy, the tributaries must be monitored so that they cannot pollute the river; they must also be damned with only the appropriate amount of water released into the main flow of the river. Some organizations are implementing separate teams that look over data quality and integration specifically. This is also a niche area that some supplier firms are beginning to fill for their clients. *Finally*, one group (distributed or centralized) should contain an aggregation of highly trained analysts that are able to take the river of information and make sense of it all. These same folks are the storytellers and the leaders that are able to guide necessary change in the internal culture; and impact the external strategy of the organization.

Business Unit (BU) Alignment

The quickest way to embed the insights function within the BU is to make the insights team directly accountable to the business unit leadership. This type of scenario allows direct access to BU decision makers and fuses product development and marketing directly with any research. In this environment, each BU has its own research budget and funds its own research separate from other BUs. The budgets, therefore, are somewhat fluid and there may or may not be a specific allocation of dollars for insights projects. That is, the insights manager may or may not have autonomous budget dollars.

Where BUs are profit centers rather than investment centers[18], there is a tendency to look at insights expenditures

---

[18] Footnote: This discussion assumes that the BU is a profit center rather than an investment center, but the distinction is an important one since it will impact the balance between strategic foresight research and tactical research. A CPG company may act more as a conglomerate and each BU is treated as a separate company; thereby it is an investment center. In this case, the insights manager embedded directly in the BU has strategic foresight responsibilities. In a technology firm, the BU may be treated as a profit center and the embedded market insights manager will likely have a more tactical focus. In such organizations, there is a need for an insights-management overlay that looks after strategy and potential synergies of the broader portfolio.

from a cost perspective rather than from an investment perspective. As such, the budget allocation leans towards more tangible and objective information sources such as the behavioral analytics; rather than commissioning more strategic research. Newly commissioned research needs to be substantiated in an ad-hoc manner by defining clear outcome metrics or specific returns on the research spend. If there is not a readily accessible ROI argument, as is often the case, then the research is less likely to be commissioned.

Advantages of the BU alignment are that insights managers are often much more pragmatic; they are closer to the BU's databases and have a more integrated view of the business. In this way, the embedded insights manager can forge strong bonds with the business managers and may be accepted more as 'one of the team'; a critical part of producing actionable insights.

The downside, especially for the cost-conscious BU, is that the lack of a strategic viewpoint can lead to mostly tactical insights being commissioned and created. For instance, the research portfolio here may be weighted towards things like product feature tradeoff, rather than research like brand identity, looking into new markets, or company-wide portfolio integration opportunities.

Strategic Planning Alignment

Here, the insights team has a direct reporting line into a strategic planning function, a corporate business development function, or into the C-suite itself. The insights function supports broad-based decisions on things such as merger and acquisition activity and corporate brand initiatives. The insights manager in this environment is usually a strategic thinker and an outstanding analyst. In fact, the *uberanalyst* described throughout this book provides a description of the ideal profile of this manager. The department may have an autonomous budget, but depending on the specific set up, the budget may be married with the overall business and competitive intelligence group.

The strength of this set up has to do with the strategic viewpoint and close communication with the highest level decision-making body of the organization. Research and strategy are one in the same and therefore the value of the research is unquestioned.

On the other hand, this centralized insights team may be somewhat removed from the decisions that managers are making on a day-to-day basis.

Matrix Structure

In this final structure, the direct reporting line is up through a corporate marketing function, but the insights function holds an autonomous budget and its own objectives. At the same time, there are dotted lines associated with the different business units and corporate functions, and the individual insights managers are assigned accordingly.

Ideally, this matrix structure provides the best of both worlds. Insights managers are able to gain specific industry and category knowledge and they can directly translate and communicate the needs of the BUs into a formal and high-quality-insight approach. While representing the BUs, the insights manager provides feedback into companywide tracking programs and can leverage other corporate initiatives to provide a wide-lens analysis for the BU. Other insights managers are assigned to *centers of excellence* where they focus on particular types of insights and act as expert consultants in these areas.

The downside of this structure is that it is sometimes criticized as creating a divisive company culture. The critique can often come from BU managers suggesting that the value-for-money proposition is no good. They complain that they contribute too much, or that another BU receives the lion's share of benefit from research initiatives which everyone must fund. Another critique is that centralized insights managers are not close enough to the front lines to understand the real needs of the BU and that research dollars are therefore wasted on providing less than useful information. While this critique has been valid to some degree in the past, and may still be valid for less data driven cultures, the insights-driven culture will, by necessity, break down these walls between the BUs and the corporate function in order to drive the organization forward.

Chapter 5- The Insights Supplier

> An agency is 85 percent confusion and 15 percent commission.
> - **Fred Allen**

Currently, Tim has three major tracking programs with three different suppliers. He hasn't formally bid out his tracking programs in a number of years because he's always felt that once you find good partners, you stick with them; and he has prided himself on being fair and loyal with his suppliers. Lately, however, he has started to feel as if at least one of his suppliers is taking advantage. The program costs have not been reduced for three years and that doesn't seem right given all the advancements in technology. Furthermore, the supplier has gone through a lot of change over the last couple of years and his contact point has changed a number of times.

Tim thinks to himself: *We need to get some fresh perspectives on our approach to all of these studies. At a minimum, we're going to have to strip some of the bloated programs down and see what social media can do for us. Perhaps we can even combine some of the studies.*

As Tim starts to call back some of the people that have been leaving him messages, he is finding that they fall into two camps.

He classifies them in his mind as either strategic firms or software firms. Interestingly, the two types of firms seem to be represented by two different types of sales people. The software oriented approaches and tools are generally represented by more junior people. The strategic firms are generally represented by a more serious person; someone that Tim can relate with.

Tim decides to push down the first round of evaluations to Becky, a detail oriented research manager who they just hired out of business school. He suggests to Becky that she work with Sanjit and the purchasing department in the evaluation process. His instructions are to narrow the set down and then set up presentations for the finalists.

Soon the presentations are set. Tim is amazed at what a great job Becky has done with the process and Sanjit is also singing her praises. She really seems to understand the situation and what they need from their next-generation supplier. Tim finds the presentations very interesting and the firms are actually quite different. This surprises him.

His notes reflect his impressions:

Firm 1: "Big Market Research Firm"

• *Some very smart people here (company big hitters). Good alignment, especially on the retail side. Significant data collection capabilities. Cost projections seem low. Still can't figure out their structure. Who's the overall owner of my program?*

Firm 2: "Management Consulting Firm"

• *Impressive big-picture thinking. Addressing Big Data and predictive modeling very well. Really seem to know our business. Outsourcing for data collection. Very expensive.*

Firm 3: "Hard to Classify Firm"

• *Mid-size firm, but very solid thinking. End-to-end approach. Using unified EFM software. Addressing Big Data nicely. Includes learning systems and data dissemination strategies. Some outsourcing. Unknown entity. Need to check these guys out.*

Firm 4: "Software Firm"

• *Impressive look and feel. User friendly. Modern technology. EFM system. Community knowledge and orientation. Per-seat-license pricing. Knows technology integration. Not really addressing Big Data beyond web-scraping. Lack true research expertise. Seems to be least expensive option, but would need to be careful with contracting.*

Firm 5: "Incumbent 1"

• *Knows our business and players well. Will reduce and combine sample frames to reduce costs. Volume discount with more business. Interesting ideas on combining the different studies with them.*

Firm 6: "Incumbent 2"

• *I wonder if they know how serious we are. Hitting hard on the switch costs. Yes, high switch costs. Suggesting sample reductions. Not rethinking the program.*

Firm 7: "Incumbent 3"

• *Couldn't meet this week.*

*****

The Market Insights supplier will need to move upstream into a strategic role, develop and sell a niche software, become the low-cost provider, or abandon the business altogether. The space that many firms have successfully occupied, that of a full-service generalist, is a failing model unless the firm can provide the service at the lowest cost or can move into strategic-partner relationships. Unfortunately, what many of these firms are encountering are shrinking margins and a clientele focused on fast-and-cheap research. At the same time, adjacent industries such as management consulting and technology firms are smelling blood in the water and swimming furiously to enter the space. This is creating a more crowded market and a promise of further industry consolidation. With this Darwinist backdrop, there are likely three models of differentiation, or some combination of the three, that suppliers will adopt: Strategic Partner Model, Software Provider Model, or Low-cost Provider Model[19].

Choosing a Direction

Strategic Partner Model

The strategic insights provider may take one of two approaches. One is a firm that acts as a general contractor knowing the best-of-breed solutions across a variety of measurement tools and suppliers. These firms will enable a

---

[19] Note that in at least one case, the software-provider model, an entirely different go-to-market strategy is needed versus the traditional full-service firm. Different go-to-market supplier strategies are discussed later in the chapter.

seamless network to serve a company and will become more important as the business intelligence side of the house begins to work more closely with the traditional research function. These firms provide a holistic viewpoint and have a clear end-to-end implementation model or business process map for multiple types of measurement systems. As traditional Market Research firms move laterally into this space with their competencies in analytics and research, they will likely encounter management-consulting firms and technology consulting firms moving into the same space.

Alternatively, the strategic insights partner may provide value by being niche focused. Unlike, the generalist firm, these suppliers will provide very clear and specific subject matter expertise. Examples may be along the lines of data integration and quality control, or pricing and forecasting. These niche approaches will be accompanied by specific vertical industry knowledge as well. The key is that the value emphasis will start to be more focused on the category expertise and outcomes and less on the research or data itself (unless the data quality and integration focus is the core offer). An example of this trend is in the category of secondary research. Due to the explosion of data and information sources around the web and the crowding of this space in general, firms that supply data-only[20] will likely become relatively less valuable than the firms that provide data-driven consulting guidance (e.g. IDC, Gartner, or Forrester in the technology industry).

---

[20] Footnote: This refers to data that can be reproduced or substituted with similar data from another source.

Software Provider Model

As sample and data collection becomes commoditized, software is becoming the backbone of the insights industry and software driven firms are becoming more numerous. These tools are coming to market in many shapes and sizes, from basic text-analytics software to fully serviced Enterprise-Feedback-Management (EFM) systems. The solutions can be integrated or point products, but they all have one thing in common: they are undercutting the traditional Market Research firms on price and forcing many industry players to change positions.

The software model itself changes how services are priced. Insights services have traditionally been priced on a project basis whereas the software industry generally prices on a seat license or on a per-processor basis. Such models ensure consistent revenues and continuous emphasis on investment in software development. In contrast, the traditional insights model is a professional services model with its high labor costs and per-project pay back. The glaring difference is that software firms run heavier up-front investment costs, but much lower operating costs. Once they have the software developed (and paid for) they are able to undercut the traditional insights supplier significantly.

Low-Cost Provider Model

The low-cost supplier model appears to split into a couple of camps, but the two share similar traits such as reducing overhead, outsourcing and off-shoring as needed, and the aggressive use of technology. These companies are finding a way to do research at a very low-cost and still produce an 'okay enough' result.

The first low-cost provider model is one of scale and is generally the domain of the large provider that already has an aggregation of global work and can speak of their global alignment and capacities. These firms are pursuing low-cost strategies by being extremely aggressive on project pricing (often coming in at a 20%+ discount to other major providers), and off-shoring and outsourcing non-critical job components. For instance, a couple of the major Market Research suppliers have pursued low-cost strategies by outsourcing data collection and analytics activities to overseas companies. Some have gone so far as to spin off call-centers, calling them non-core services; only to turn around and rethink the decision. These firms seem to be gaining traction as they win share, but the strategy comes at a cost. The strategy to 'never lose on price' is putting margin pressure on the entire Industry and has created something of a deflationary scenario for research consultancies.

The second camp of low-cost suppliers are the smaller, more nimble providers that have very low overhead to start with and are helped tremendously by advances in technology and the commoditization trend in the sample business. In recent years, the barriers to entry have come down to a level where strong industry veterans with a good network can step out and start a firm on their own. The basic infrastructure of a data collection and reporting software platform, a decent sample provider, and a statistician (if the principals aren't building their own models), provides the equivalent of a start-up business in a box. If one needs to provide ethnographic research, a learning system, or unique info graphics, these contract services and software tools are easily available as bolt-on offers.

Organizing for Success

The canopy of the insights industry includes many different branches of the value chain such as consulting and professional services, data collection and sample access, secondary data market, and increasingly, technology integration capabilities. Different support functions are often provided in-house within a major supplier, or completely outsourced by a small start-up supplier. For these reasons, it's hard to put forth a one-size-fits-all model to address the different suppliers. Instead, the attempt here is to set out some general models and go-to-market approaches based on the firm's specific market offer.

Classic Consulting Model

The classic consulting model is a natural fit for the purely professional services organization and is the de-facto model in most law firms, traditional-consulting firms, and accounting firms. In the insights industry, this structure is ideally suited for a firm whose advantage is based in niche knowledge and employs a project based approach (i.e. more ad hoc studies rather than tracking studies, syndicated work, etc.). The structure is generally a partnership with the most senior consultants sitting on top of their respective pyramids. In this position, they act like their own CEO with operational, as well as new business development, responsibilities. As the organization grows, more levels are inserted into the pyramid and the junior partners start to manage their own book of business; thus, they begin to build their own hierarchy. The traditional consulting model may look something like what is outlined below in Figure 3.

Figure 3: Classic Consulting Model

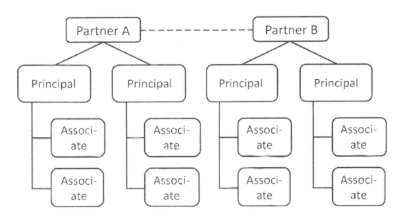

The strength of this model is that resources are generally focused on one agenda, and advancement opportunities and career paths, or lack thereof, are relatively clear. There is no tension between a business development team (tasked with acquiring new customers) and the client services teams (tasked with implementation) since everyone is part of the same hierarchy. The client also knows exactly who they are speaking with in terms of organizational level, and by and large, roles and responsibilities are clearly understood to all involved.

On the downside, there may be issues to scale this model if the senior partner has a hard time 'letting go' of clients and feels the need to oversee every detail of his organization. Resource utilization can be an issue as well if one group is busy, but another group is not. This is particularly true where organizational communication is weak or one partner has a hard time sharing their underutilized resources. Furthermore, if the client becomes dissatisfied with the service, there is usually only one escalation path and no alternate avenues for the firm to resolve client issues. Finally, there can be significant productivity issues if powerful senior partners decide to face off against each other.

Matrix Model

The difference between the matrix services organization and the traditional consulting model is that, in the matrix model, the account managers have client service and business development responsibilities, but they each draw from an indirect resource pool of program or project managers; rather than managing those resources directly. These resources likely report through an operations department or COO, and have only a dotted line to the account managers. A basic representation is presented below in Figure 4.

Figure 4: Matrix Organization

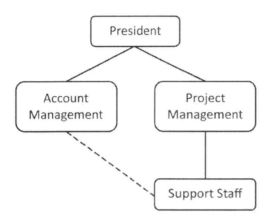

The strength of this model is resource utilization as the pool of managers is shuffled around based on demand. Individuals get to work on a variety of projects and exposure across industry or project type is much more prevalent. This model seems to work better for tracking study businesses since the operations, technology and quality control (imperatives for a good tracking study) can often be managed better within the domain of operations. The model is also quite scalable assuming good communication between account managers and their project management counterparts. Client escalation of issues can be easier to handle, but again this depends on solid communication between the two departments.

On the downside, lack of communication and trust between the operations side and the primary client services team can spell disaster for the organization if the two groups start to fight at the expense of the client. If this does happen, the client becomes dissatisfied with the lack of communication and confused on whom they should approach in order to resolve the issue. The other risk with this type of model is that employees may get discouraged by the lack of career growth; though this attitude may be correlated as much with the type of work as with the organizational structure (i.e. tracking work versus ad-hoc work).

Business Development Models

On the operational side, the Business Development (BD) model may be similar to the matrix model or the traditional consulting model, but the distinction for the BD model is that there exists a separate department primarily responsible for on-boarding new accounts. Hunting versus farming is an oft-used analogy. The two groups, operations (a.k.a. client service) and BD can be peer groups that report to executive management of the company (e.g. the company president) or BD may report to a partner or client services.

The BD model works well if an organization has high growth targets (e.g. demand creation is a primary focus) or if the offer is more transactional based (e.g. off-the-shelf software sales where the design and client service team isn't as integral to the offer). The overall BD model may be further broken into two-types which might be called "Subordinate BD" and "Prominent BD" (See Figures 5 and 6 below). The downside of either BD model is that it can be resource intensive. If the company does not align expectations appropriately, or if the company does not subsequently begin to see significant revenue growth, profitability will suffer.

SUBORDINATE **BD** MODEL

Figure 5: Subordinate BD Model

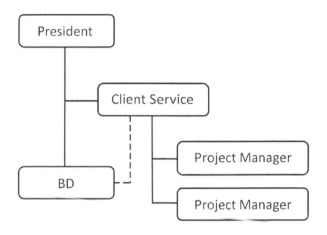

The Subordinate BD model is more akin to a direct sales force model where sales people are valuable in terms of prospecting new accounts and managing the sales process, but they generally control no resources and are somewhat powerless within the context of the broader organization. In the Market Research world, these are the door openers, but seldom the actual door closers. The reason for this is that they generally do not own the design of the research program and unless one owns the design, it's very difficult to negotiate the complexities of the deal. Furthermore, their perceived value to the client may be as grease in the machine. This is not to say that introductions and the sales process management is not key for success, but the client does not perceive the value to them of the Subordinate BD person; rather the client feels that they are buying the services of those individuals providing the program thought leadership and the overall program design.

PROMINENT BD MODEL

Figure 6: Prominent BD Model

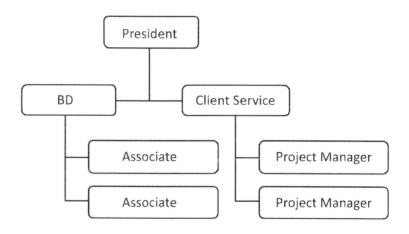

In the Prominent BD model, the business developer is usually a multi-faceted industry veteran and is fully empowered by the organization to bring on what one might call the 'new' logos. These insights professionals excel in matching business needs with a research solution. Such business developers take part in key management discussions so that they can adequately represent the company, but also so that they are able to directly represent the voice of the marketplace to management. Other roles might include oversight of key relationship building campaigns, presenting leading ideas at industry conferences, and designing client programs. In order to do this, the company culture puts the business developer in a role of thought leadership. It isn't to say that others in the organization are not providing thought leadership, but the business developer is well respected in representing the best thinking of the organization. In terms of process, the Prominent BD manager takes the lead role in on-boarding the account and securing a trusted relationship between the two organizations. Once such a relationship is established, there is handoff to another senior-level manager on the client service team.

Chapter 6- The Insights Professional

> An expert is someone who has succeeded in making decisions and judgments simpler through knowing what to pay attention to and what to ignore.
>
> - **Edward de Bono**

Every step of the way, Tim's been consulting Gabrielle and Lucas regarding the direction he is taking the Market Research department (which has now changed its name to Market Insights and Analytics). They have been very supportive. His initiatives have also caught the attention of Joe, the COO. After some back-room discussions with Lucas and Gabrielle, Joe suggests a reallocation of budget so that Tim can hire more analysts. It seems to be a more natural fit than to put these folks on Gabrielle's team. Lucas and Gabrielle agree.

Tim thinks about his staff. He has a couple of what he considers big picture analysts on the on the team now, but he needs to hire more. Luckily, his meetings with Gabrielle have really paid off, and Lucas has really shown support as his boss. He now has the green light to hire some analysts, but the skill set is going to be hard to find: Industry knowledge, modeling knowledge, computer savvy, and an ability to deliver compelling executive reports.

A real uberanalyst, Tim thinks to himself. *Becky was a great hire, perhaps the best I ever made. The business school program she came out of has a real interdisciplinary approach. Not only can she write well, but she has a solid analytics background and she's technology savvy. I bet with what's going on with Wall Street these days, there are a lot of MBA types looking for jobs...*

*****

Only when the enterprise extracts wisdom from the data can they hope to gain true advantage, yet this extraction is still a markedly human function. With business intelligence and Big Data coming to the forefront of the organization, the rare individual with a mix of statistical knowledge, computer savvy, category knowledge, and creative storytelling becomes the organizational star. On the flip side, any manager uncomfortable with data runs the risk of becoming marginalized within the new polity. Of course, the knowledge of statistics, economics, computers, and specific industry are just an ante[21]. The successful analyst understands human behavior, the corporate political environment, critical information sources in the organization, and where each of these fit. And there's more. The successful analyst will exhibit a multi-disciplinary approach and invoke creative storytelling to deliver compelling reports and reveal actionable insights. Given the lengthy list here, the focus in this chapter is on those skills

---

[21] Given the many books written on these topics, these skill-sets are not further addressed in this book. It should suffice to say that an intermediate to advanced understanding in each of these areas are foundational to success in the market insights industry.

that go beyond the ante and provide true professional differentiation.

Understanding the Layers of Market Insights

Integrating information from multiple sources is a hot topic in the insights world and it has been for many years. As with a work of art, no matter the focal point, it's the context that often gives as much information as the subject itself. With the proliferation of Big Data, the context becomes much more animated and competes to become subject matter itself. Regardless of the derivation of the data, however, one should be able to look at any particular initiative like a new advertising campaign or product introduction and relate it to the broader business metrics. Often discussed in terms of return on marketing investment (ROMI), this linkage can be the impact on revenue or profit, or impact on less tangible metrics such as brand equity, customer loyalty, or employee engagement. A holistic insights framework provides a common insights language across the organization and there is less need to constantly re-educate staff on metrics and models; perhaps most importantly, it gives senior analysts the ability to look at the entire picture and assess return on marketing investment (ROMI).

Figure 7: Layers of Insights (Key Below)

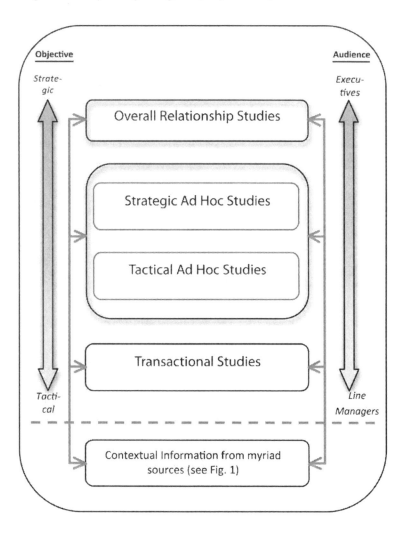

Key to Figure 7:

Relationship Tracking Studies	e.g. Brand Equity, Customer Loyalty, Employee Engagement, etc.
Strategic Ad Hoc Studies	e.g. Market Structure, Segmentation, Forecasting, Opportunity Assessment, Market Sizing, Brand Position (a.k.a. Brand Identity/Brand Promise), New Product Innovation, Market Mix Optimization (Promotion Portfolio), Line Optimization (Product Portfolio), etc.
Tactical Ad Hoc Studies	e.g. Copy testing, Product Evolution, Mystery Shopping, Sales-Force Effectiveness, etc.
Transactional Tracking Studies	e.g., Call center, On-line/Brick-and-Mortar Retail transactions, Sales Win/Loss, etc.
Contextual Data/Business Intelligence Systems	All data from internal and external sources used to feed and enhance models

The depiction above is kept as simple as possible. The layers represent different aspects of the research function and the company's core business intelligence networks are presented as the contextual frame for the picture. In this sense, the business intelligence system represents all the data that is available to frame the issue, feed the analysis, and link operational and financial results. Once organizational leaders are aligned, the tactical implementation involves the creation of common metrics that act as bonds across studies and information. These can be anything from linking similar demographic, behavioral or psychographic profiles, to simply placing a small battery of common questions in survey instruments.

Overall Relationship Studies

The top layer represents strategic information such as brand equity and overall customer relationship metrics. Depending on the organization, different stakeholders such as channel partners, employees, or investors may need to be tracked as well. These scores may represent individual metrics such as Net-Promoter Score (NPS)[22], or could be some sort of brand index that looks at multiple metrics. Some models tie in harder metrics such as profitability or revenue directly into the index. The audience for these metrics is often higher level managers and executives since these are lagging indicators that necessitate longer planning horizons. Much like the financial manager has tools such as balance sheets, income statements and financial audits; the insights manager has his own set of tools. In the case of the relationship studies, the executive may think of these strategic studies as the balance sheet for the assets and liabilities of key stakeholder relationships.

---

[22] Footnote: See Sidebar Discussion: Individual metrics versus indexes for overall Relationship Measurement

Sidebar Discussion: **Individual metrics versus indexes for overall Relationship Measurement**

Net Promoter Score (NPS) was made famous by Fred Reichheld in his Harvard Business School article, entitled "The One Number You Need to Grow". In this article, he presents his argument that the willingness to serve as a referral source for the brand is closely tied with revenue growth. The beauty of this theory is that a single number, such as a NPS, is easily implemented and understood, and it serves as an actionable rallying point to garner political support and mobilize human resources in the organization.

(Continued on following page...)

> *The other side of the debate has been argued persuasively by people such as Tim Keininghan of Ipsos. The counter-argument, and its associated research, suggests that a single number is not the best predictor because multiple metrics will always outperform. Intuitively, this argument is hard to ignore as we would expect that convergent information would provide better answers.*
>
> *There is no right or wrong approach; rather there is a tradeoff to make. It is a similar tradeoff that must be made many times in market insights function: To what degree does simplicity and action-ability take precedence over the quality and depth of the research results.*

Ad-Hoc Studies

Ad-hoc studies can be strategic or more tactical in nature, but in a well-integrated system they often grow out of the findings of the bigger picture relationship tracking studies. On the strategic side, such ad-hoc studies include market structure, brand identity, segmentation, or market-mix models. On the tactical side, they can include studies such as product evolution, or sales-win loss analysis. Depending on the nature of the research being conducted, the audience for these metrics can be anywhere from line-level managers to senior-level managers.

Transactional Studies

The bottom layer encompasses all the customer touch-points or *moments-of-truth* that represent the interactions with a company's brand. These metrics are leading indicators that represent the executional excellence of an organization and will eventually show up in the more strategic metrics such as brand equity scores. From a survey perspective, the study is generally called a trailer survey, an event-based survey, or a transaction survey. These studies often look at outcome metrics associated with a particular encounter with the organization; be it through a call center, a web site, or a face-to-face experience. The internal audience for these metrics is line level managers who are empowered to take immediate corrective action. The manager may think of these tactical studies as their day-to-day operating statement for valuable customer interactions.

Driving Successful Initiatives

Funding Your Initiative

The key to getting funding for the initiative is to think like the program stakeholders. Since the money in the organization flows down from the top, one should be well versed in the executive agenda and try to align goals and objectives with the overall corporate strategy. If there is a pet project belonging to a relevant higher-level executive, figure out a way to tie in that initiative. (If there is no direct access to top-level decision makers, one can read SEC filings and look closely at the company intranet to get information. This information can be communicated to the team and the folks that do have contact with upper management.)

Make sure to speak with any accessible stakeholders early in the process so they feel that their voice is heard. In particular, the people that are funding the project need to be closely regarded in this process. The key is to design the project around what people actually need rather than what is often only a perceived need on behalf of the researcher.

Once the executive interviews are done, quickly sketch out an informal one page plan that is not technical but user-friendly from a management perspective. This can be as simple as stating the background for the program (i.e. the why), the objectives and expected outcomes of the program (i.e. the so what), basic approach and resource requirements (i.e. the how), timing (i.e. the when), and cost (i.e. the how much). Make sure the plan is described in terms of ROI. If ROI linkage is not readily available, one can focus on the importance and value of the business decision that the insights will support.

Depending on the circumstance, a good idea is to break the program up into small chunks. For instance, a small piece of qualitative work can show the value of a larger initiative. It can create excitement around the program and sometimes result in more funding. This is especially true if there is only partial funding at the start of the initiative.

Finally, don't go after every project opportunity since every initiative cannot be financially backed. The risk of presenting too many initiatives for consideration is that 'no' becomes the more common answer to the funding question. On the other hand, if a new program is well chosen, well thought out, and well communicated, it will likely get funded most of the time.

Addressing the 'So What' Question

If the question of research value is posed to insight managers and business managers separately, they are likely to give different answers. The research staff will claim high value of research, while the business manager may suggest that research has less value. Some of this disconnect between the two groups can be attributed to the inherent self-interest of the insights managers to promote the value of their work. More importantly, the insights information is often disregarded due to a lack of business context or a lack of understanding of the real priorities of the organization. Regardless of who is at fault, the most damning outcome of the lower-valued research is that it never answers the critical business question, *so what*?

In order to address this challenge, the insights manager and the business manager must start with a common understanding of the business questions; or if the effort is more exploratory in nature, what type of questions are to be created. In order to do this, the insights managers must proactively engage their internal audience in an honest and informed dialogue. This is where initiatives often fall short as the insights managers get into a room with their internal stakeholders and wait for those stakeholders to tell them what to do. Instead, the successful insights manager takes the proactive role of creating the agenda and driving the discussion around the goals of the initiative; a smart move given that the ultimate responsibility for project success or failure will often be given to the insights manager. This is not to say that the insights managers are responsible for creating the business objectives; rather they are acting more as a strategic facilitator who draws out the objectives from the audience and artfully focuses the group on the possible outcomes.

Another key to success, and key to answering the 'so what' question, is to always make sure the objectives address specific business outcomes rather than just existing in-and-of themselves. As long as there is buy-in from the business managers on the objectives and business outcomes, and the initiative is executed well, then the 'so what' question will be answered.

Setting Appropriate Expectations

High quality, on time, and on budget are the hallmarks of a successful insights manager, but oftentimes insights initiatives fail to deliver against these criteria. Consistently achieving these objectives can often be attributed to the ability and experience of the insights manager; if the insights manager communicates clearly and effectively then they have a much higher probability of success. This is especially true if the initial expectations are not being met.

Timelines

Long time horizons on research studies, especially those requiring multiple waves and a longitudinal analysis, often present real challenges for business managers. In the technology industry, a new product may already be in market and certain information rendered useless if it isn't delivered in a timely manner. This should be a non-starter if the research program takes too long, but some insights managers feel compelled to underestimate the project timeline and just get the research done. This often ends up in a bad situation where much of the project time is put into data collection and the most important time allocation (i.e. up-front due diligence and reporting) is reduced significantly. While the research may get completed, it is often of the lower quality field and tab variety.

To address this situation, make sure the methodology matches the timeline; there are often multiple ways to get what you need. If results are needed in three weeks, skip the primary research and figure out an alternative methodology (e.g. web-scraping or secondary data sources). Use the advice of Enrico Firme who suggested that measurement isn't about certainty; rather it's about reducing uncertainty. Some information is better than no information, and perfect information is useless if it doesn't arrive in time.

You can also break initiatives into shorter projects. For a project including significant qualitative and quantitative work, each phase may have separate timelines and deliverables. This keeps stakeholders engaged and informed during the time it takes to complete a long project. For larger and presumably more important initiatives, it is important to break out the due-diligence phase and try not to make any hard commitments until that phase is completed. After all, it is difficult to establish budgets and timelines until one knows the complete scope of the project.

Budgets

Budget is another area of missed expectations for insights managers. Unexpected events in the field, unexpected programming hours (especially with projects involving software implementation), quality issues, or possibly extra hours needed for analysis and reporting can create an over budget situation. The insights manager is often stuck between not delivering the intended results and going back to ask for more money.

There are a few ways to make sure everyone is on the same page in terms of budget and that there are no surprises. First, make sure to ask if the budget is in place before getting the project going. The worse thing that can happen is to get through the design phase, and just before implementation, the budget is cut for the project.

Sometimes, the design phase is really just a pitch for project funding and there won't be any dollar allocation until people are convinced that the program will get them what they need. In this case, it's important for the insights manager to know that the program is still being marketed internally and that it's not yet completely viable. It is also important to communicate this with any suppliers. The key is to talk about money up front and be clear on what people may or may not receive given their budget parameters.

The insights manager should also be clear about what the project covers and does not cover and puts aside a contingency budget of approximately 10% to cover unexpected expenses (or more if there is an unproven supplier in the picture). This will usually cover things such as change orders with suppliers and other issues that may arise. If the money is still there toward the end of the project, the extra budget can be used for such things as additional value-added analysis or refunding the money to the stakeholder.

Data Quality

Data quality is another important issue in terms of expectation setting since data quality is often considered an underlying expectation. To use the poker analogy, data quality is table stakes. With that said, there can be serious issues that need to be addressed in order to make sure the data set is defensible.[23]

The perception of quality, timeliness, and staying within budget are all impacted by how adeptly the insights manager sets expectations and the level of trust established with the internal client. Part of this credibility is gained for the insights manager through their knowledge of which tool is right for the job, and experience in terms of time, money and pros and cons of different approaches. For example, if a qualitative technique or a crowdsourcing technique will work in lieu of a higher priced and longer quantitative study, then the insights manager can point that out and gain respect. It's this foundational guidance as well as hitting the big three

---

[23] Footnote: Perception of quality includes both data quality as well as insights quality. Developing quality insights are addressed earlier and later in the chapter. Please see: *"Addressing the 'So What' Question"* and *"Delivering Impactful Reports and Compelling Insights"*

performance metrics (budget, timing, and quality) that earns the trust and develops a reputation of a solid insights manager.

Delivering Impactful Reports and Compelling Insights

The first consideration when delivering an insights report is always the internal audience and what they are hoping to accomplish. This starts in the earliest due diligence period of the study. When engaging in the initial needs analysis discussions, it is imperative that the objectives are clearly defined and well informed.

A good start to this process is to discover two or three critical business questions that would have significant business impact if they were answered. A business outcomes statement should also be included in which specific results of the research are clearly articulated in a short paragraph. This may be thought of as something of a mission statement for the work. Note that many times, internal audiences will ask for the world, but only have a shoe-string budget. In this case, it is the job of the insights manager to corral expectations and make sure the final objectives are not only possible, but fruitful.

For primary research initiatives, the study objectives and business questions should serve as the flagships for the data collection instrument; the key to a successful initiative. For example, the insights team should be able to quickly map each question in a survey instrument back to a particular business objective. This keeps the "must haves" separate from the "nice to haves" and is a particularly helpful process when survey 'real estate' is in short supply.

The story itself and how it is presented is one of the most critical factors for success. The use of info graphics and creative storytelling can help tremendously, but it is a process to get there. A simple skeleton outline of the story flow and content can be created and presented to the stakeholders for reaction well prior to final report delivery. This step can not only save a lot of rework, but can often be the difference between ultimate project success and failure. Comparisons to other companies of interest in the industry (benchmarking) as well as exploring specific customer examples are often useful and can add a lot of color. This is where in depth qualitative research and videography can help as well. In terms of structuring the report, the 101 business approach is often the best. Tell them what you are going to tell them, tell them in detail, and then tell them what you just told them. It is important to note that while the storyline may be the same for everyone in the organization, it is often necessary that insights managers customize the message for different audiences. For example, a Vice President will often just want the 'top line', whereas the line manager responsible for the business may want to look at all the detailed information. It is important to have two different pitches for these audiences. Finally, at any given time, the insights manager should be ready with a 30 second verbal synopsis of the storyline. Often called an elevator pitch, this executive summary comes in handy all over the organization (not just in elevators).

It is imperative to understand that the report information must be disseminated through the organization for the initiative to be successful. The insights manager should not shy away from working closely with the communications team and business managers to make sure this happens. In fact, as corporate communications and insights starts to converge, the insights manager may increasingly be involved with driving the communications and the learning systems that are a critical part of insights initiatives.

Ultimately, the amount of time spent in the due diligence phase and in the reporting phase should account for a disproportionate amount of project time. This enables the focus of the research to be on things such as gaining initiative support, defining clear and concise reasons for the research, and making sure the underlying message is delivered in an impactful way.

Conclusion - Time to Take Your Seat

> Action speaks louder than words but not nearly as often.
> - Mark Twain

Tim sits at his desk and thinks about how much his department has changed in just a year. He remembers the same time last year when Gabrielle brought in the Business Intelligence consultancy that helped US Telco solve part of their churn issue, and how his budget had faced dramatic cuts. While his team is still in the process of changing from one of a support team to a real advisory role within the organization, things are definitely headed the right direction. It seems every key decision the company is making comes across his desk for feedback at some point. More impressive is that his department has established an impressive track record over the last number of months. Profitability and revenues are both increasing, and the company is starting to gain significant share.

Tim thinks about how he got to this point. He had taken two risks, both of which had paid off. The first was to push hard to make sure that information analysis and interpretation resided in his department. He had worked with Gabrielle on a joint task force to make this happen; Business Intelligence training was now a key part of the department curriculum and his group owned almost all information interpretation and analysis. The task force had also installed organization-wide protocols for making market decisions.

The second risk was going with the new supplier that had originally impressed him at the presentations and had opened his eyes to the importance of disseminating information internally. The company not only understood the Big Data and market research aspects, but they were able to bring in best-of-breed solutions for info graphics and video production; even learning systems implementations were under their umbrella. These things were integral in helping to create the behavior change he needed within the organization. There is now a cadence that is sounding through the corporate hallways, and US Telco is quickly being recognized for its *best in class* approaches to Market Insights.

Tim sits, considering the work he and his team have done and how much the market research industry has changed.

He thinks to himself, *I wonder what the industry will look like in another twenty years...*

*****

The thing with disruptive change is just that...it is disruptive. Things are fine...until they are not. It is business as usual for some time as industry foundations change, but then it happens. If the reader takes away nothing else from this book, it is this: Disruptive change is occurring in the Market Research industry and for those who get it, they will adapt and prosper. For those who just see things as business as usual and they write off budget decreases or project holds to the economic downturn, they will ultimately suffer.

The new ethos will call for a breaking down of the walls between insights and an organization's information-technology capabilities. A juxtaposition of the two cultures of technology and Market Research shows what a formidable task this may be for the Market Research traditionalist: Technology is fast where Market Research is slow; software is cheap where Market Research is expensive; technology is good enough, where Market Research is precise; with technology, change is constant, with Market Research, it is episodic. Unfortunately for the unchanging organization, the software model that focuses measurement on fast, cheap, and good enough, is what many corporations are asking for these days.

Advancements such as cloud computing, artificial intelligence, social networking, and on-line communities threaten commoditization of key parts of the Market Research industry. This trend can be seen in the empowerment of corporate purchasing departments that take control of the traditional Market Research function and treat it as nothing more than a cost center. Whatever supplier attribute that can be put into a spreadsheet and ranked, will be. While there are a number of different components for major survey programs (e.g. data collection, incentive management, questionnaire design, analytics, reporting, etc.), substitute data sources, new technologies, and the perception of simplicity have allowed the corporate purchasing department to move into a position not only of procurement manager but also that of Market Research program manager. The role provides value by componentizing the research and utilizing low-cost insourcing, outsourcing, and off-shoring approaches as needed.

On the strategy side, companies are more likely to insource strategic value-added roles than to grant confidential access to outside firms. In the cases that companies do let in consulting firms to fill more strategic roles, this access will be based on the consultant's ability to see the entire picture, not just a piece of it. Such consultants will be able to bring in the right partners for the right insights initiatives, integrate and analyze many sources of information, and most of all, provide true strategic insight and 'best practices'. Outside of this role as general contractor, the value of the insights consultant will revolve around any unique data they may possess, a particular software application, a differentiated niche research approach, or expertise in data quality control and integration.

The good news is that the Market Research industry is in a unique position to provide the leadership needed to move forward into this brave new world of analytics. More and more, organizations will follow the sage advice of Peter Drucker, who famously said "that which gets measured, gets done", and measurement is the core skill of the researcher. The question is who in the Market Research industry will step up to the plate and take a swing. Change is always a formidable task, but certainly not an impossible one. Firms need to look to the business intelligence world and systems integration experts to help them bring forth the power of big data. Only those that look beyond the research itself and ground themselves in knowledge of *all* available data will fulfill the charter.

The differentiator for both internal and external insights providers are the individuals that make up the team. It is the unique human ability of the highly skilled researcher to ask exactly the right questions and build a compelling data-driven business case. So much comes down to the individual with a rare mix of statistical knowledge, computer savvy, category knowledge, and creative storytelling. Emphasis will be on the ability to not only put together different methodological approaches, but to put together a compelling story. Once the story is complete, the analyst must be able to navigate deftly through the interior of the organization to make sure the correct story is heard. It is this interdisciplinary skill set that will drive tomorrow's insights function. We're seeing this in the types of people being recruited for the market insights role and in how business schools are preparing their students. For corporate-group managers, the goal will be to put together a team of these *uberanalysts* that work well together, not just as lone wolves. In the successful organization, such uberanalysts will have the ability to extract wisdom from the cornucopia of data; and it's this voice that will be heard before the intuition of other managers. Such analysts will become high-ranking executives in the organization as information management and market insight is viewed as an investment center delivering competitive advantage.

The Market Research industry can take advantage of all of the trends put forth in this book because it has been nourished by a cross-pollination of many different disciplines and the fundamental link is curiosity. Asking questions and putting ideas together is a core competency of the industry and a critical competitive advantage for today's corporation. Many industry analysts have significant skill sets with important software such as SAS or SPSS, and others are trained in such things as ethnography and storytelling. Most importantly, the research industry contains a vast pool of educated, information-savvy, interdisciplinary professionals. The industry provides opportunities to those interested in both art and science; and such is the renaissance profile of today's uberanalyst. And this is the profile of the 21st century Market Insights leader.

CPSIA information can be obtained at www.ICGtesting.com
Printed in the USA
BVOW02s2350181015

422952BV00001B/113/P